D1577586

Dr Johnson, His Club and Other Friends

Jenny Uglow

Published in Great Britain by National Portrait Gallery Publications,
National Portrait Gallery, St Martin's Place, London WC2H 0HE

ISBN 1 85514 232 5

A catalogue record for this book is available from the British Library

Series Project Editors: Celia Jones and Lucy Clark
Series Designer: Karen Osborne
Series Picture Researcher: Susie Foster
Printed by PJ Reproductions, London

Front cover:
Samuel Johnson (1709–84)
Sir Joshua Reynolds, *c.*1756 (detail)
Oil on canvas, 127.6 x 101.6 cm
© National Portrait Gallery (1597)

For a complete catalogue of current publications,
please write to the address above.

Contents

❦

SAMUEL JOHNSON, James Heath after Sir Joshua Reynolds, 1756
Frontispiece to the first edition of Boswell's *Life of Johnson*, 1791

INTRODUCTION

❧

Joshua Reynolds's first portrait of Samuel Johnson (1709–84), painted around 1756, just after the publication of Johnson's *Dictionary*, signalled a change in the direction of British culture. Genius and learning, Reynolds suggested, no longer resided solely with aristocrats and connoisseurs, but could be found in a large, plain, bourgeois man, lost in thought, seated on a plain chair, his papers on the table beside him, his pen at the ready. When this portrait was engraved as the frontispiece for Boswell's *Life of Johnson* in 1791 Johnson was smartened up, given buttons on his waistcoat and a ponderous frown. Further gravitas was added by the uncovered table and the volume clearly titled JOHNSON'S DICTIONARY A–K. This was the image that Johnson's followers wished posterity to see: meditative, imposing and utterly authoritative.

Johnson's influence came not only from his own work but from his collaboration with overlapping circles of friends: the set who enjoyed the Thrales' hospitality at Streatham, the female 'Bluestockings', the theatrical world of David Garrick (1717–79), the university dons of Oxford, the provincial coteries of his home town, Lichfield, and the most influential group of all – the 'Literary Club', which flourished from the 1760s to the 1790s.

'Man is a sociable animal and we take all occasions and pretences of forming ourselves into those little nocturnal assemblies which are commonly known as *clubs*', Joseph Addison had written in the *Spectator* in 1711. His tongue-in-cheek list noted Ugly Clubs, Farters' Clubs, Flirting Clubs and Surly Clubs, but more serious clubs existed for every calling, from politicians and philosophers to musicians and artists. Often based in coffee-houses or taverns, they created powerful informal networks outside the state and the official institutions.

JOSEPH ADDISON
Sir Godfrey Kneller, before 1717

Pre-eminent among the early clubs was the Kit-cat Club, promoting Whig politics and culture, whose members included Congreve and Vanbrugh, Addison and Steele – and Sir Godfrey Kneller, whose long series of Kit-cat portraits hung in the house of the publisher Jacob Tonson. Kneller's portraits transformed seventeenth-century court style into a new look, at once intimate and assured, urban and urbane. The Kit-cats, self-elected rulers of British taste and opinion, confront the viewer with an open gaze while remaining distinctly aristocratic.

In the eighteenth century Britain was well known, even laughed at, for its obsession with portraits. They were commissioned for all significant events – birthdays, weddings, the inheritance of estates – turned out on almost factory-like lines by leading painters, often with several assistants. Portraits were a conscious and complex form of self-display. To convey the appropriate refinement, Jonathan Richardson insisted in *The Theory of Painting* in 1715, the artist's duty was 'to raise the Character; to divest the unbred person of his Rusticity, and give him something at least of a Gentleman'. Sitters should be 'good actors' and artists must give them the air required 'when one comes into Company, or into any Publick Assembly, or at the first sight of any particular person'.

Appearances counted. But if appearance was all, how could portraits convey inner character? In the portraits of Johnson and his circle a shift in tone is immediately apparent. The courtly style lingers in images of landed members like Topham Beauclerk (1739–80), James Boswell (1740–95) or Joseph Banks (1743–1820). But unlike the Kit-cat Club, most members of the Literary Club were not aristocratic or wealthy: Johnson's father was a bookseller, Reynolds's an apothecary, Garrick's a soldier, Edmund Burke's a Dublin attorney. Lack of money and mounting debts were often the greatest spurs to their creativity. But they still aspired to greatness, and their portraits reflect this, proudly depicting a new, bourgeois intelligentsia.

The Club valued talent and vision above status or political allegiance. It began informally in 1764, when Joshua Reynolds (1723–92), anxious about Johnson's growing depression, suggested founding a group where his great talent for conversation could flourish. Originally there were eight members: Johnson and Reynolds, Edmund Burke (1729–97) and his father-in-law Dr Christopher Nugent, Oliver Goldsmith (?1730–1774),

Sir John Hawkins (1719–89), the Huguenot financier Anthony Chamier and Johnson's two younger friends Topham Beauclerk and Bennet Langton (1737–1801). According to Thomas Percy (1729–1811), a later member, numbers were kept low because, 'It was intended the Club should consist of Such Men, as that if only Two of them chanced to meet, they should be able to entertain each other sufficiently without wishing for more Company with whom to pass an evening'. At first they met weekly at the Turk's Head tavern in Gerrard Street, Soho, where they had a light supper at seven and talked on, as Boswell said, 'till a pretty late hour'.

In the 1770s the Club grew larger and more formal, with fewer meetings. In addition to Boswell, Percy and Garrick, new members included the historian Edward Gibbon (1737–94); the musician Charles Burney (1726–1814); the new managers of Drury Lane George Colman (1732–94) and Richard Brinsley Sheridan; the linguist Sir William Jones; the Shakespearian editors Edmund Malone (1741–1812) and George Steevens; and leading politicians such as Charles James Fox and William Windham. Among other luminaries were Adam Smith, elected in 1775, a year before publication of *The Wealth of Nations*, and Sir Joseph Banks, President of the Royal Society in 1778. Numbers rose, finally limited to thirty-five in 1780. Glumly, Johnson saw his Club heading towards being 'a mere miscellaneous collection of conspicuous men'. But these conspicuous men were immensely influential. For the first time a rich body of inherited and new British culture was formulated and systematised; in Johnson's

CHARLES JAMES FOX, Joseph Nollekens, *c*.1791

ADAM SMITH, James Tassie, 1787

Lives of the Poets (1779–81), in Hawkins and Burney's histories of music, in Percy's ballads and Malone's Shakespeare, in Gibbon's narrative of Rome, in the economics of Adam Smith and the botanical work of Banks.

The Club's fame ensured that its members were represented in a whole range of media, from full-scale oils and bronze busts to Wedgwood medallions. Over the years Reynolds painted more than twenty Club members. He endowed them with dignity but stressed their humanity, blending their respect for 'Reason' with the new vogue for 'Sensibility'. His portraits were often engraved as frontispieces to their works, one example of the endless Club collaborations.

If the Club was exclusively male, Johnson's wider circle was not. He was long dependent on the clever and devoted Hester Thrale (1741–1821), and was friendly with several remarkable women from the learned Elizabeth Carter (1717–1806) to the novelists Charlotte Lennox (*c.*1720–1804) and Fanny Burney (1752–1840), and the 'Bluestockings' who flourished under the patronage of rich hostesses like Elizabeth Montagu. But eminent women posed problems for painters: their individual portraits all fall into current 'feminine' conventions and only Anna Seward (1742–1809) is portrayed as literary. By contrast to the men, when such exceptional women are celebrated as a group, they are not placed informally round a table. Instead, in Richard Samuels's *The Nine Living Muses*, exhibited at the Royal Academy in 1779, they are tactfully translated into classical idiom.

The evident contrast between male and female portraiture is, however, not nearly as sharp as that between the images of the Club created by

The Nine Living Muses of Great Britain: Portraits in the Characters of the Muses in the Temple of Apollo, Richard Samuel, exhibited 1779

From left to right: Elizabeth Carter; the painter Angelica Kauffman (seated); the essayist Anna Letitia Barbauld, the singer Elizabeth Linley (centre; wife of Sheridan); feminist and historian Catharine Sawbridge Macaulay (with scroll); Elizabeth Montagu (centre of seated trio); Hannah More (with text); and behind them Elizabeth Griffiths, the Irish actress, and the novelist Charlotte Lennox.

admirers and those drawn by sceptical outsiders. Their cultural dominance and incestuous air of mutual self-congratulation often roused ridicule. Some caricatures are affectionate, like *The Artist's Studio*, by an unknown artist in the style of Thomas Patch, or Reynolds's own caricatures painted in Rome in the 1750s. Others were harsher: the satiric poet Charles Churchill dubbed Johnson 'Pomposo' in the early 1760s, a name used with great effect in James Gillray's later satires. Club members who were also prominent politicians, like Edmund Burke, inevitably provoked

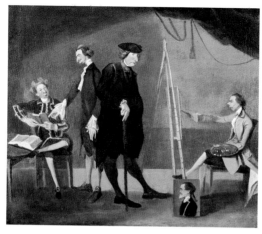

The Artist's Studio
Unknown artist,
*c.*1760–70. Dr Johnson,
Bennet Langton and
Topham Beauclerk in
Sir Joshua Reynolds's
studio

caricatures, but the group as a whole could seem ludicrously self-important, and works like Boswell's *Tour of the Hebrides* (1786) provided irresistible material: Samuel Collings produced twenty drawings, engraved by Rowlandson as *Picturesque Beauties of Boswell*. After Johnson's death in 1784 the rush to record his life roused intense mockery, typified by Soame Jenyns's tart epitaph in the *Gentleman's Magazine* of 1786:

> *Here lies poor Johnson: reader have a care;*
> *Tread lightly, lest you rouse a sleeping bear.*
> *Religious, moral, generous and humane*
> *He was; but self-sufficient, rude and vain;*
> *Ill-bred and overbearing in dispute;*
> *A scholar and a christian and a brute.*
> *Would you know all his wisdom and his folly,*
> *His actions, sayings, mirth and melancholy,*
> *Boswell and Thrale, retailers of his wit,*
> *Will tell you how he wrote and talked, and coughed and spit!*

The fuss that surrounded Johnson, his Club and his friends, serves to measure the degree of their importance, both to their age and to posterity. They are introduced in this book roughly in the order in which they came into Johnson's life, but the portraits included here emphasise their individuality and variety, as well as their solidarity and strength.

SELECT BIBLIOGRAPHY

G. Birkbeck Hill, ed., *Johnsonian Miscellanies*, 2 vols., Oxford, 1897.

J. Brewer, *The Pleasures of the Imagination: English Culture in the Eighteenth Century*, London, 1987.

J. D. Fleeman, *The Correspondence of James Boswell with Certain Members of the Club*, London, 1976.

Abraham Hayward, ed., *Autobiography, Letters and Literary Remains of Mrs Piozzi (Thrale)*, 2nd edn., 2 vols., London, 1861.

Sir John Hawkins, *The Life of Samuel Johnson, LLD.*, 2nd edn., London, 1787.

G. B. Hill, ed., *Boswell's Life of Johnson*, revised and enlarged by E. F. Powell, 6 vols., Oxford, 1934–64.

W. Jackson Bate, *Samuel Johnson*, London, 1978.

Samuel Johnson, 1709–84, bicentenary exhibition catalogue, Arts Council of Great Britain, London, 1984.

The Journals and Letters of Fanny Burney, ed. Joyce Hemlow, 12 vols., Oxford, 1984.

The Letters of David Garrick, ed. D. M. Little and G. M. Kahrl, 3 vols., London, 1963.

L. Lipking, *The Ordering of the Arts in Eighteenth-Century England*, Princeton, 1970.

S. H. Myers, *The Blue Stocking Circle: Women, Friendship and the Life of the Mind in Eighteenth-Century England*, Oxford, 1990.

J. Northcote, *Life of Sir Joshua Reynolds*, 2 vols., London, 1818.

N. Penny, ed., *Reynolds*, exhibition catalogue, Royal Academy of Arts, London, 1986.

M. Pointon, *Hanging the Head; Portraiture and Social Formation in Eighteenth-Century England*, New Haven and London, 1993.

Sir Joshua Reynolds, *Discourses on Art*, ed. R. R. Wark, New Haven and London, 1975.

A. Robinson, *Edmund Burke, A Life in Caricature*, London, 1996.

D. Shaw-Taylor, *The Georgians: Eighteenth-Century Portraiture and Society*, London, 1990.

Thraliana: The Diary of Mrs Hester Lynch Thrale (later Mrs Piozzi), ed. K. C. Balderston, 2nd edn., 2 vols., Oxford, 1951.

R. Wendorf, *The Elements of Life: Biography and Portraiture in Stuart and Georgian England*, Oxford, 1990.

R. Wendorf, *Sir Joshua Reynolds: The Painter in Society*, London, 1996.

SAMUEL JOHNSON, Sir Joshua Reynolds, 1769

SAMUEL JOHNSON (1709–84)

Samuel Johnson was a literary giant – lexicographer, critic, novelist, poet and biographer. But while admirers praised his reason and moral judgement, his rolling prose and stirring conversation, others saw him as a dictator, rounding on opponents with a ferocious 'No, Sir!' He was prone to deep melancholy but capable of great gusts of laughter: Fanny Burney decided that 'Johnson has more fun, and comical humour, and love of nonsense about him, than almost anybody I ever saw'. Johnson knew himself well: 'Have you not observed', he asked Mrs Thrale, 'that my genius is always in extremes; that I am very noisy, or very silent; very gloomy, or very merry; very sour, or very kind?'

Reynolds's second portrait of Johnson suggests this inner complexity. Although the model is classical, the effect is almost shocking, and there is a foretaste here too, of the inspired, near-mad 'Romantic' genius. It is often called '*Dr Johnson arguing*', but the argument is internal. The hazel eyes are closed in a slight squint and he is gesticulating fiercely, as he often did, Reynolds said, when he was left out of conversation and his mind appeared to be preying on itself. Reynolds's sister Frances bears witness to the realism: 'his gestures with his hands', she wrote, were very strange, sometimes he would hold them up with some of his fingers bent, as if he had been seized with the cramp, and sometimes at his Breast in motion like those of a jockey on full speed.'

Samuel Johnson was born in 1709, in Lichfield, just north of Birmingham, the son of a bookseller who ran into financial troubles. As a small child he contracted scrofula, which left him almost blind in one eye and near-sighted in the other, with oddly twitching limbs. After a classical education he worked in his father's bookshop before a small legacy enabled him to go to Pembroke College, Oxford, but oppressed by his poverty, he was, he said, 'rude and violent' and left in 1729 without a degree.

In Birmingham, in 1735, Johnson disconcerted friends by marrying the widowed Elizabeth Porter: she was forty-six, with three children; he was twenty-five. But Tetty loved his learning and conversation, and with her financial help, he started a school. When this failed, in 1737, Johnson set off for London. For the next few years he worked for Edward Cave's *Gentleman's Magazine*, a 'Grub Street hack', publishing his great poems *London* (1738) and *The Vanity of Human Wishes* (1749), and the *Life of*

TETTY JOHNSON, unknown artist, *c.*1734

Savage (1744), and planning his 'New Dictionary of the English Language'. To support himself he wrote the eloquent essays in *The Rambler*, and to enjoy himself formed his first club at the King's Head in Ivy Lane, whose members included Arthur Murphy, Sir John Hawkins and John Hawkesworth.

Tetty, who never liked London, began drinking heavily. When she died in 1752, a remorseful Johnson plunged more fiercely into work on the

Dr Johnson in his Travelling Dress, Thomas Trotter, 1786

great *Dictionary*, published in 1755. Yet he despaired at his laziness, claiming to write only for money: to solve his debts he wrote the light-hearted essays *The Idler* (1758–60); to pay for his mother's funeral he wrote his philosophical novel *Rasselas, Prince of Abyssinia* (1759).

A royal pension eased his fortunes after 1760, and from 1764 he found security, friendship and scope for conversation in the Club. To Johnson, talking was an art and a combat. 'He fought on every occasion,' said

Reynolds, 'as if his whole reputation depended upon the victory', but Goldsmith, often his victim, decided that 'Johnson, to be sure, has a roughness in his manner; but no man alive has a more tender heart. He has nothing of the bear but his skin.'

In 1765 Johnson's eight-volume edition of Shakespeare was finally published, but years of hard work had exhausted him; in 1766 he suffered a near breakdown and was nursed by the Thrales at Streatham. Yet, despite frequent illness, he was more than ready to undertake the strenuous three-month tour to the Hebrides with Boswell in August 1773. Johnson's time was always full. He resented the hours wasted, apparently, on sitting for his bust to Nollekens in 1777. Nearly all his friends – including Mrs Thrale and Frances Reynolds – objected to this powerful likeness, especially to the hair, complaining that in attempting to depict him like an ancient poet, Nollekens had made him more like 'a sturdy, long-haired Irish beggar'. James Barry's forceful, intimate sketch dates from around the same time.

SAMUEL JOHNSON, Edward Hodges Bailey, 1828, after Joseph Nollekens, 1777

SAMUEL JOHNSON, James Barry, *c.*1777. Oil sketch made for *The Distribution of Premiums*, in his series of murals, *The Progress of Human Culture*

Johnson's last great project sealed his fame. 'I am engaged to write little Lives', he told Boswell, 'and little Prefaces, to a little edition of the English Poets.' His readable, lucid, pioneering *Lives of the Poets* were published between 1779 and 1781. Yet his spirits were low. The break with Mrs Thrale over her marriage to Gabriel Piozzi in 1782 left him deeply downcast, and in early 1784 he suffered a heart attack. He recovered and formed a last, small club which met in Essex Street. But a long journey to Lichfield and Oxford, returning in a freezing November, left him ill again. Before his death on 13 December 1784 he wrote his moving last prayers. At Johnson's funeral in Westminster Abbey, Banks, Langton, Burke and Colman were among the pall-bearers and Reynolds, Hawkins, Burney, Strahan and Malone were in the congregation. The Club bore him company to the last.

ANNA SEWARD, Tilly Kettle, 1762

ANNA SEWARD (1742–1809)

The poet Anna Seward, 'the Swan of Lichfield', knew Johnson in his youth but was no wholehearted admirer: she called him 'the imperious and gloomy Intolerant', and told anecdotes of him 'with great humour, and with a very striking imitation of the sage's peculiar voice, gesture and manner of delivery'. Her dislike was partly anger at his treatment of old connections, and partly a profound disagreement over taste: where he was a professional metropolitan critic, a Tory and an upholder of reason, she was an amateur, a proud provincial, a reformer and a devotee of sentiment.

The daughter of a scholarly clergyman, Seward was a child prodigy, famed for reciting *Paradise Lost* and composing metrical psalms. In the 1780s, after publication of her *Elegy on Captain Cook* and *Monody on Major André*, she was determined to be taken seriously as a critic, writing in periodicals like the *Gentleman's Magazine*, stoutly defending the melancholy, lyrical poets of her day, Gray, Collins, Cowper and Burns.

In 1784 Seward published *Louisa*, a highly successful verse novel of ill-fated love. Deeply romantic, she rejected several proposals but developed passionate attachments, especially to her friend Honora Sneyd, who married Richard Lovell Edgeworth and died young, and later to John Saville, the cathedral singer (as he was a married man this caused some scandal). She could seem over-emotive but had great generosity and style: as this fine literary portrait suggests, Seward was tall and elegant; she had auburn hair and brown eyes which seemed, said Sir Walter Scott, to 'become darker and flash fire' when she was animated. Her uninhibited, opinionated letters appeared in 1810.

DAVID GARRICK (1717–79)

❧

The actor, playwright and theatre manager David Garrick, responsible for transforming the British stage in the mid-eighteenth century, was a great self-publicist. He loved having his portrait painted, and there are innumerable images of him in paint, pencil, pastel and engraving, on playing cards and medals, in theatrical costume and gentleman's pose.

One of the most charming of men, 'Davy' was the first pupil at Johnson's school and they left Lichfield together in 1737. His father, a soldier, came from French Huguenot stock; as a boy, he served a short apprenticeship to his uncle, a Lisbon wine merchant, and in London he and his brother Peter started a wine business. He also wrote for the *Gentleman's Magazine* after Johnson introduced him to Edward Cave, and his sketch *Lethe* was performed at Drury Lane in 1740. Garrick burst into the limelight himself as Richard III at Goodman's Fields Theatre in 1741.

David Garrick as Richard III, William Hogarth, 1745

Hogarth's dramatic painting of him in this role, terrified by the ghost's appearance, brilliantly conveys the impact of his new, naturalistic style, and also heralded a whole new genre of theatrical portraiture.

Garrick's triumphs continued in comedy as well as tragedy, and in 1747, when he joined James Lacy in managing Drury Lane, Johnson wrote the celebratory prologue: repaying the favour, Garrick staged Johnson's *Irene* in 1749. As a manager, Garrick's great mission during the next decades was to refine the British stage, known for its boisterous audiences and its medley of drama, farce and cheap pantomimes. He met resistance as well as praise, and in 1763, weary of the capital, left for the Continent, where he was given the Freedom of the Comédie Française, returning with revived energy in 1765. Although he wrote his own plays, collaborating with George Colman in comedies such as *The Clandestine Marriage* (1766), Garrick always stressed the art of the actor, rather than the text. 'Speeches and poetry will no more make a Play', he told Boswell in 1772, 'than planks and timbers in the dock-yard call be called a Ship – It is Fable, Passion & Action which constitute a Tragedy, & without them, we might as well exhibit one of Tillotson's Sermons.'

Above all, Garrick was largely responsible for the new cult of Shakespeare. He staged his own adaptations – sometimes near travesties – built a Shakespeare temple in his garden on the Thames at Hampton, collected early editions, and created the 'Shakespeare Jubilee' at Stratford-on-Avon in 1769, a spectacular success when restaged at Drury Lane, ending with rousing choruses, firing guns and ringing bells.

Yet despite, or perhaps because of, his passion for Shakespeare, Johnson kept him at arm's length. Publicly Johnson acknowledged Garrick's talent, but privately he damned his vanity and name-dropping: 'Dr Johnson', said Reynolds, 'considered Garrick his property, and would never suffer any one to praise or abuse him but himself.' When Garrick heard of the Club from Reynolds, he allegedly said, 'I like it much; I think I shall be of you'. *'He'll be of us?'* retorted Johnson, 'How does he know we will *permit* him?' Until 1773 he barred Garrick's membership, because 'he will disturb us by his buffoonery', and when Boswell quizzed him, he asked scornfully what 'merit' could be due a man who 'claps a hump on his back, and a lump on his leg, and cries *"I am Richard III"*?'

Garrick was as proud of his status off stage as on, and the fine double portrait of 1773, with his wife, the delightful Viennese dancer Eva Maria Veigel, known as La Violette, shows him as the epitome of the polite gentleman. Garrick made his last stage appearance in June 1776; when he died three years later he left a huge fortune, a superb library of rare books, prints and play-texts, and a fine collection of paintings. When he was buried in Westminster Abbey the coaches stretched 'from Charing Cross to the Abbey'. 'I suppose he had more, what we may call particular friends, than any man in England', said Hannah More. Despite the tension between them, Johnson was spotted standing by Garrick's grave 'bathed in tears'.

DAVID GARRICK AND HIS WIFE EVA MARIA VEIGEL
Sir Joshua Reynolds, exhibited 1773

THE PUBLISHERS

EDWARD CAVE (1691–1754)

Publishers were vital figures for this circle, and Edward Cave gave several their first chance. A Midlander from Warwickshire, educated at Rugby Grammar School, Cave had several odd jobs, including being a printer's apprentice and reporter, before buying a printing house in 1731 and founding the *Gentleman's Magazine*, which he edited under the pseudonym Sylvanus Urban. A huge success which inspired many imitations, this was published from St John's Gateway, Clerkenwell, for over fifty years. For six years, from 1738, Johnson wrote for the magazine, where fellow-contributors included Richard Savage, John Hawkins and Elizabeth Carter. A shrewd, thoughtful man, always to be found in his office, Cave could seem slow and apathetic but was in fact highly inventive and energetic. Charles Grignion engraved this memorial portrait, with its quotation from *Paradise Lost*, after Cave's death, probably for circulation among his friends rather than as a frontispiece.

EDWARD CAVE, Charles Grignion, *c.*1754

ROBERT DODSLEY (1703–64)

Dodsley was an unusual and powerful character. His first poem, 'Servitude', was written while working as a footman, but by 1735 he had become a bookseller, and soon a playwright; his *Select Collection of Old Plays* (1744) was an invaluable compendium and several of his own plays were successfully staged. An innovative bookseller–publisher, well known for his sponsorship of poetry, he published Johnson's *London* (1738), *The Vanity of Human Wishes* (1749) and *Irene* (1749), and was later the co-publisher of *Rasselas* (1759) with William Strahan. It was Dodsley who suggested the idea of the *Dictionary* to Johnson in 1746. In 1758, prompted by Edmund Burke, he founded the *Annual Register*, and with his brother James published Goldsmith's *Polite Learning* the following year. The portrait here suggests a man proud of his achievement, a tough, neat, humorous, determined soul.

ROBERT DODSLEY, attributed to Edward Alcock, ?1760

WILLIAM STRAHAN, Sir Joshua Reynolds
Exhibited 1783

WILLIAM STRAHAN (1715–85)

Reynolds's powerful portrait, exhibited at the Royal Academy in 1783, shows Strahan as a man of strong character and alert intelligence, utterly trustworthy, as his friends knew him to be. Born in Edinburgh, he came to London in 1738 and rapidly rose to become a wealthy printer and publisher. Eventually, his titles ran from Tobias Smollett's *Roderick Random* (1748) and *Peregrine Pickle* (1751), to Lawrence Sterne's *Tristram Shandy* (1759–67), Henry Mackenzie's influential *The Man of Feeling* (1771), Adam Smith's *Wealth of Nations* (1776) and Edward Gibbon's *Decline and Fall of the Roman Empire* (1776–88). In 1770 Dodsley was made the King's Printer, and in 1774 became an MP. He printed Johnson's *Dictionary* and virtually became his manager, being linked to nearly all Johnson's later works. Strahan administered Johnson's pension and sometimes acted as his banker, handing over much needed advances when he was in difficulties.

ELIZABETH CARTER (1717–1806)

Elizabeth Carter's father, the curate of Deal Chapel in Kent, was determined that her education should equal her brothers', teaching her Latin, Greek and Hebrew. She learnt French and taught herself Italian, Spanish and German, and some Portuguese and Arabic (to sustain herself, she allegedly wrapped a wet towel round her head, took snuff and chewed green tea). To cap this, she studied mathematics, geography, history and astronomy, and played the spinet and the flute.

Her father's friend Edward Cave published her poems in the *Gentleman's Magazine* under the pseudonym 'Eliza' when she was seventeen, and her *Poems upon Particular Occasions* appeared in 1738. Johnson, a fellow contributor, was charmed by her mix of scholarship and shyness. 'Poor dear Cave,' he wrote to her later, 'I owe him much, for to him I owe that I have known you.' Johnson composed a Greek epigram to her, and the magazine carried his verses 'To Eliza plucking Laurel in Mr Pope's Gardens' (they were working jointly on a Swiss critique of Pope's *Essay on Man*).

Highmore's elegant portrait shows the unassuming muse in rich modern dress, with a laurel wreath being prepared for her in the background. Her major work was the translation of Epictetus, published in 1758. Later she contributed to *The Rambler*, published more poems and was a noted member of the Bluestockings. Religious but independent, rejecting marriage and careless of fashion, she stuck to a vigorous daily routine, despite caring for her father's large family by his second wife. Her combination of domesticity and scholarship prompted Johnson's notorious tribute, 'Mrs Carter can bake a pudding as well as translate Epictetus, and work a handkerchief as well as compose a poem'. A venerated old lady, Carter died aged eighty-nine, outliving Johnson by over twenty years.

ELIZABETH CARTER, Joseph Highmore, *c*.1745

SIR JOHN HAWKINS (1719–89)

A lawyer, musician and writer, John Hawkins met Johnson when Hawkins, a London carpenter's son, now articled to an attorney, began writing for the *Gentleman's Magazine* in 1739. While Johnson was immensely sociable, Hawkins was staid, precise and blunt – 'a most unclubbable man', said Johnson. His works included an edition of Walton's *The Compleat Angler* (1761); he also wrote plays, and was implacably resentful when Garrick turned them down, but his greatest achievement was his *General History of the Science and Practice of Music* (1776). The portrait by James Roberts was commissioned by Dr Philip Hayes, Professor of Music at Oxford. Hawkins seems to be holding a novel, but against the ranged volumes of his *History* he presents a conventional, stern, sunken-mouthed image; his daughter hated the picture, declaring that he was 'painted as he never looked, dressed as he never dressed, and employed as he never was employed'.

Hawkins rose to become a Middlesex magistrate. He never had much money and was often thought mean. One of the original and most unpopular members of the Club, he withdrew because of an argument with Burke, yet was one of Johnson's most loyal friends; as his executor, his one error was the hasty sale of Johnson's vast library. In 1781 he published his *Life*, issued with the first major collection of the *Works*. Although Boswell disliked the 'dark uncharitable cast' of this memoir, it represented Johnson, thought Elizabeth Carter, 'impartially, and very decently and candidly'.

SIR JOHN HAWKINS
James Roberts, 1786

JOHN HAWKESWORTH (1715–73)

The journalist John Hawkesworth took over Johnson's Parliamentary debates for the *Gentleman's Magazine*, and later followed up Johnson's *Rambler* with his own twice-weekly series entitled *The Adventurer*. A clever adapter of Johnson's style, he was one of the members of Johnson's first club, in Ivy Lane.

Hawkesworth had a mixed career as journalist, playwright and poet. He collaborated on several productions with Garrick, was the biographer and editor of Swift, and produced a compilation of the journals of James Cook and Joseph Banks, *An Account of a Voyage round the World* (1773). At one stage both Johnson and Reynolds called him a 'coxcomb', but in his portrait Reynolds placed him reverently before his book-lined shelves, quill in hand. Despite his reservations, Johnson remained a close friend, declaring that his poems showed 'a very powerful mind', although regretting that he was one 'whom success in the world had spoiled'. After Hawkesworth's death Johnson began compiling (but never finished) an edition of his works.

JOHN HAWKESWORTH
James Watson after Sir Joshua Reynolds, 1773

SIR JOSHUA REYNOLDS (1723–92)

Sometimes called Britain's greatest portrait painter, Sir Joshua Reynolds was the instigator of the Club, recording its members in acute, perceptive character studies, particularly in the portraits commissioned by Henry Thrale for Streatham Park.

Born near Plymouth, in Devon, the third son of a vicar and teacher, Reynolds was apprenticed in 1740 to the painter Thomas Hudson, a fellow Devonian. He was stylish and ambitious, and in the youthful painting of 1747–9 wears fashionable informal dress in brown and blue, and his own curly hair instead of a formal wig. This self-portrait is the only one in which he shows himself actually painting. He looks innocent, almost anxious, but his gaze seems to go beyond the imagined sitter, peering into the distance, the future, the dreams he hopes to fulfil.

SELF-PORTRAIT, Sir Joshua Reynolds, c.1747–9

In 1749 he accompanied Commodore Keppel to the Mediterranean, and spent three years studying in Italy. (A cold, caught while painting in the Vatican, triggered his lifelong deafness.) On his return, Reynolds rapidly became the most sought-after London portraitist, using the powerful naval portrait of his patron Keppel as a demonstration piece, and painting heroic full-length portraits, nobles in van Dyck dress and elegant images of fashionable women. Although he had assistants, his work-load was stupendous, and his prices rose sharply. In 1760 he moved to a large house in Leicester Fields, his home until his death.

Many of Reynolds's portraits were grandiose works, but he could also produce intimate, affectionate likenesses and Johnson grieved that he should 'transfer to heroes and goddesses, to empty splendour and to airy fiction, that art, which is now employed in diffusing friendship and renewing tenderness, in quickening the affections of the absent, and continuing the presence of the dead'. The two men met around 1755 and quickly became friends. Reynolds claimed that Johnson 'may be said to have formed my mind, and to have brushed off from it a deal of rubbish'. Johnson, in turn, admired Reynolds's 'habit of thinking for himself', and often quoted from his *Discourses* in later editions of the *Dictionary* to define terms like 'gentleness', 'glow', 'nature', 'portrait' and 'style'. At his darkest moments in 1764, the year that Reynolds suggested founding the Club, Johnson thought of him as 'almost the only man whom I call a friend'.

Reynolds was enormously significant in raising the status of British artists. In three essays for *The Idler* in 1759, he claimed that painting was an intellectual, not a technical activity; 'for the painter of genius cannot stoop to drudgery, in which the understanding has no part; and what pretence has the art to claim kindred with poetry, but by its powers over the imagination'. These essays were also part of a campaign to found a Royal Academy, for which artists had pressed since the 1740s. In 1768, when the Royal Academy finally received its charter, Reynolds was elected its first President, and was knighted in 1769. From now on he poured much of his energy into the Academy, developing his aesthetic ideas in annual *Discourses*. In 1784 he was appointed Painter in Ordinary to the King.

Reynolds is sometimes presented as a dull, rather pompous character, yet he was kindly and immensely gregarious, keeping a touch of his

SELF-PORTRAIT, Sir Joshua Reynolds, 1788

Devon accent and never wholly polished in manner. Despite his deafness he belonged to many clubs, was 'much addicted to the tavern', a great playgoer and a lively host. Many of his friends were literary and theatrical (among other things, he contributed notes to Johnson's *Shakespeare*).

Towards the end of his life his eyesight began to fail. Malone thought the honest and moving self-portrait of Reynolds wearing his spectacles was 'exactly as he appeared in his latter days, in domestick life'. Still full of vitality, this elderly image offers a touching contrast to the youthful, far-seeing self-portrait. In 1790 Reynolds abandoned painting and gave his last *Discourse*; when he died, in February 1792, he was buried in St Paul's Cathedral.

CHARLOTTE LENNOX (*c.*1720–1804)

Born in Gibraltar, where her soldier father was stationed, after an adventurous youth, in 1747 Charlotte Ramsay married Alexander Lennox, an impoverished Scot who worked for William Strahan. To solve their debts Lennox acted and wrote, publishing *Poems on Several Occasions* (1747). At this point she met Johnson, whose Ivy Lane club arranged 'a whole night spent in festivity', to celebrate her first novel, *The Life of Harriot Stuart* (1750): Johnson later wrote publishing proposals for her, dedications and even parts of her novels. Declaring his admiration for Elizabeth Carter, Hannah More and Fanny Burney, he pronounced, 'Three such women are not to be found: I know not where I could find a fourth, except Mrs Lennox, who is superior to them all'. All four appear in *The Nine Living Muses*, from which this detail is taken.

CHARLOTTE LENNOX, detail from *The Nine Living Muses of Great Britain: Portraits in the Characters of the Muses in the Temple of Apollo*, Richard Samuel, exhibited 1779

Charlotte Lennox worked relentlessly, but is chiefly remembered for *The Female Quixote* (1752), a burlesque romance about a young girl's introduction into society. After translating Voltaire's *The Age of Lewis XIV* (1753), she compiled the three-volume *Shakespeare Illustrated* (1753–4), published still more translations, plays and novels and edited her own journal *The Lady's Museum* (1760–61). Lennox's later years saw much sadness: her daughter died, she separated from her husband and her son had to emigrate to America. After her final novel, *Euphemia* (1790), Lennox relied on a pension from the Royal Literary Fund, and she died, penniless, in Westminster in 1804.

JOSEPH BARETTI, unknown artist after Sir Joshua Reynolds, 1773

JOSEPH BARETTI (1719–89)

Guiseppe Marc'Antonio Baretti (anglicised as 'Joseph') was the son of a Turin architect, who arrived in London in 1751, aged thirty-two, and opened a small school. Charlotte Lennox introduced him to Johnson, who felt protective to this shy, awkward yet headstrong character, and wrote a preface to his *Introduction to the Italian Language* (1755). He also helped Baretti with his *Italian Library* (1757) and wrote a dedication to his English/Italian dictionary in 1760.

Johnson respected his energy and when Baretti was abroad, from 1760 to 1766, wrote lively letters to him. In 1769 Baretti was acquitted of a murder after he stabbed a man in self-defence in a Soho brawl. At his trial Johnson, Reynolds, Garrick, Beauclerk and Burke were character witnesses, Johnson describing him as a scholar, always known to be 'peaceable' and indeed probably 'timorous'.

Johnson introduced him to Streatham where he became a regular guest of the Thrales and then, after 1773, the children's tutor in Italian and Spanish. He acted as courier on the Thrales' trip to France, and Reynolds painted his portrait for the library, portraying the thick-set, short-sighted Baretti peering at his book. In this copy of Reynolds's painting he looks almost affable, but in fact he quarrelled constantly with Mrs Thrale over her intellectual pretensions and her attitude to the children: he was angry when the Thrales' Italian tour was cancelled, and in 1776 he turned on his heel and walked out. In 1790, in his posthumously published *Strictures*, Baretti venomously attacked Hester's edition of Johnson's letters.

Baretti was a brilliant but unstable man, who often turned on those who tried to help him. When he died in 1789, poor and embittered, the *Morning Post* noted caustically that 'the death of Baretti has, perhaps, excited regret in no human being'.

CHARLES BURNEY (1726–1814)

❦

In 1755 the music teacher and organist Charles Burney wrote admiringly to Johnson concerning the *Dictionary* and their friendship began. Burney was born in Shropshire, the nineteenth child of a penniless dancing master and a portrait painter. He came to London as a pupil of Thomas Augustus Arne, published his first compositions in the mid-1740s, played in the orchestras of Drury Lane and Vauxhall Gardens and composed music for Garrick, who became a close family friend. In 1749 Burney was elected to the Royal Society of Musicians, but in 1750 left London after an illness, becoming organist in King's Lynn in Norfolk.

After he returned in 1760 Burney cleverly managed the balancing act of being a fashionable music master and a member of town society. He travelled through Europe on fact-finding trips for his *History of Music*, and in 1773 was elected to the Royal Society. Three years later, with a dedication by Johnson, came the first volume of his *General History of Music: From the Earliest Ages to the Present Period* (the fourth and final volume appeared in 1789). Burney's elegant, engaging prose has a vitality and immediacy which legitimised music once again as a serious, 'polite' pleasure.

In 1776 he began to teach the Thrales' daughter Queeney the harpsichord and soon gained extra status as the father of Fanny, author of the successful *Evelina*. He was immensely flattered when Henry Thrale commissioned Reynolds's portrait, the last of the Streatham series. The pose vividly conveys the sense of listening to unheard music, and the image suggests Burney's gentleness and eagerness while his Oxford doctoral robes add dignity – although Johnson complained, 'we want to see *Burney* and he never comes to me in that dress'.

From 1783 Burney was also organist at Chelsea Hospital, a post obtained for him by Edmund Burke, and in 1784 he was finally elected to the Club.

CHARLES BURNEY, Sir Joshua Reynolds, 1781

BENNET LANGTON (1737–1801)

BENNET LANGTON
William Daniell after George Dance, 1798

A great admirer of *The Rambler* at the age of seventeen Bennet Langton wangled a meeting with Johnson. It was the start of a long correspondence and oddly tender friendship.

Langton was the eldest child of an old Lincolnshire family. An excellent classical scholar, he met Topham Beauclerk at Trinity College, Oxford. They travelled together to the Continent, and were inseparable companions in London, where both were founder-members of the Club.

In 1770 Langton married Mary, Dowager Countess of Rothes, and eventually had ten children, whom he spoiled dreadfully. Devout, prone to talk religion at wrong moments, he was also hopelessly impractical, living expensively in London instead of on his estate. Yet he worked closely with the North Lincolnshire Militia and laboured to recoup the family fortunes as an engineer in Chatham. He was disorganised, late, absent minded, far too mild for the Club. 'Mr Langton seems to stand in a very odd Light among us', wrote Mrs Thrale, 'he is acknowledged Learned, Pious, and elegant of Manners – yet he is always a person unrespected and completely ridiculous.' Six foot four and unnaturally thin, he looked odd too, a 'very tall, meagre, long-visaged man, much resembling a stork standing on one leg', said one friend. But although he seemed comic, he aroused great fondness, as is evident from this affectionate pencil sketch.

Johnson thought him the worthiest man he knew: 'I know not who will go to heaven if Langton does not.' Langton was present at Johnson's deathbed, edited his Latin poems and succeeded him as Professor of Ancient Literature in the Royal Academy.

TOPHAM BEAUCLERK (1739–80)

The great-grandson of Charles II and Nell Gwyn, grandson of Charles Beauclerk, 1st Duke of St Albans, Topham Beauclerk was introduced to Johnson by Bennet Langton and also became a close friend of Reynolds and Garrick.

The urbane engraving shown here catches something of his elegance and style, 'a man of wit, literature and fashion in distinguished degree', as Boswell called him. On the surface, Beauclerk was a fashionable dilettante; privately he was a dedicated scholar. Sceptical and arrogant, he stood up boldly to Johnson's rudeness. 'What a coalition' wrote Garrick of the Langton–Beauclerk–Johnson friend-

TOPHAM BEAUCLERK
Unknown artist

ship. But the younger men offered Johnson an escape. The best-known story tells how they once hammered on Johnson's door at 3 a.m. until he appeared 'in his shirt, with his little black wig on top of his head, instead of a night cap, and a poker in his hand'. On finding who they were, he smiled – 'What is it you, you dogs! I'll have a frisk with you.' – dressed, and went with them to Covent Garden, drank punch and took a boat down to Billingsgate in the dawn.

Beauclerk was a known rake, famed for his affairs on the Continent and in London. In 1766 Lady Diana Spencer, Viscountess Bolingbroke, left her husband (known for his own infidelities) and bore Beauclerk's child; they married when Bolingbroke divorced her. But Beauclerk's health was always poor, and pain and drugs made him, Horace Walpole said, 'the worst tempered man he ever knew . . . He took Laudanum regularly in vast quantities'. Despite his failings, when he died in 1780, aged forty, Johnson lamented that 'his wit and his folly, his acuteness and maliciousness, his merriment and reasoning, are now over'.

Arthur Murphy (1727–1805)

Murphy met Johnson in 1754. Aged twenty-seven, he was editing his own periodical, the *Gray's Inn Journal*, for which he translated an oriental tale from a French magazine, only to discover that it was an unacknowledged translation from *The Rambler*: embarrassed, he wrote to Johnson and visited to apologise. Johnson received him warmly, and he soon became his 'dear Mur'.

Murphy, the son of a Dublin merchant, was educated at Saint-Omer in France, before working as a clerk, and founding his journal. To solve debts (the inevitable spur) he began acting, playing Othello at Covent Garden in 1755, and his first play, *The Apprentice*, was staged at Drury Lane in 1756. His twenty plays ranged from farces and Molière adaptations to lively comedies of manners, like *The Way to Keep Him* (1760) and *Three Weeks after Marriage* (1764), and tragedies such as *The Grecian Daughter* (1772). He also edited Henry Fielding's *Works* in 1762, continued his journalism and qualified as a barrister.

With Reynolds, Murphy influenced Johnson to accept a pension, and in 1765, through his friendship with Henry Thrale, he arranged Johnson's

first invitation to Streatham. This fine portrait by Nathaniel Dance was supposedly painted for the Thrale daughters. Murphy could be suspicious, irascible and jealous – his relationship with Garrick was a lifelong dispute – but he was a loyal friend to the elderly Johnson, and a member of the last, small Essex Street club. His *Essay on the Life and Genius of Samuel Johnson* appeared in 1792, and his *Life of David Garrick* in 1801.

Arthur Murphy
Nathaniel Dance, 1777

GEORGE COLMAN (1732–94)

The playwright George Colman was elected to the Club in 1768, but had long been associated with the Johnson circle. He was born in Florence, where his father was a British envoy, and educated at Westminster School and Christ Church, Oxford. A good classicist, who later translated Terence and Horace, he trained at Lincoln's Inn, and was a practising barrister from 1759 to 1764. In the mid-1750s, with old schoolfriends, including Bonnell Thornton, Charles Churchill and Robert Lloyd, he was part of the 'Nonsense Club', producing the satiric journal

GEORGE COLMAN
Thomas Gainsborough, *c.*1778

The Connoisseur. Colman, however, aimed at the theatre, and his spirited, witty plays *Polly Honeycombe* (1760) and *The Jealous Wife* (1761; an adaptation of *Tom Jones*) were staged at Drury Lane. Colman was tiny, with a boy-like figure, but he was educated, talented, polished, hard-working and ambitious: from 1763 to 1765, when Garrick was in Europe, he managed Drury Lane, and their collaborations included *The Clandestine Marriage* (1766).

Gainsborough's portrait shows Colman in his late forties, a successful man of the world, resting on his considerable achievements. Unstoppably energetic, Colman wrote or adapted at least thirty plays; his comedies were unusual and influential in treating contemporary issues. After managing Covent Garden from 1767 to 1774 (where his greatest scoop was producing Goldsmith's *She Stoops to Conquer* in 1773, after Garrick rejected it), Colman ran the Haymarket Theatre from 1777 to 1789, retiring five years before his death.

THOMAS PERCY (1729–1811)

The fine portrait of Thomas Percy by Reynolds, engraved by William Dickinson, brings out his romantic streak as well as his cool, haughty reserve. He is painted in half-profile, wearing the loose velvet turban favoured by writers and artists. Under his arm he holds the heavy volume which he brought to London in March 1759, a collection of old ballads in a seventeenth-century hand, which he had found in a friend's house, saving them from a maid about to light the fire. With Goldsmith, Garrick and Thomas Warton, Johnson advised Percy on publication and his epoch-making *Reliques of Ancient English Poetry* appeared in three volumes in 1765, fostering a new interest in old poetry.

In 1764 Johnson stayed in Percy's country parsonage, and the following year he became a member of the Club. A grocer's son from Bridgenorth in Shropshire (although he claimed links with the aristocratic Percys of Northumberland), Percy graduated from Christ Church, Oxford, in 1746 and was vicar of Easton Maudit in Northamptonshire for nearly thirty years. Shrewdly in tune with current taste for the ancient and the exotic, he published translations – a Chinese novel and Icelandic verse – and as well as the *Reliques* produced other antiquarian works, notably *Northern Antiquities* (1770).

Percy was good-natured but cautious, and his refusal to be goaded into confrontations irritated Johnson. They argued fiercely at the Club in 1778 over Thomas Pennant's *Tours of Scotland*, especially when Percy dared to mention Johnson's short-sightedness. After that their friendship cooled. Percy became chaplain to the Duke of Northumberland and in 1769 to the king. In 1778 he was made Dean of Carlisle and was finally Bishop of Dromore in Ireland from 1782 to his death.

THOMAS PERCY, William Dickinson, 1775, after Sir Joshua Reynolds, 1775

EDMUND BURKE (1729–97)

For over a century, Edmund Burke's pronouncements swayed the theory and practice of British politics, defining a conservative centre that all arguments had to combat.

Writer, orator and statesman, Burke was the son of an Irish Protestant attorney. After Trinity College, Dublin, he came to London in 1750 to study law, but his interests were chiefly literary: his dazzling and provocative *Philosophical Enquiry into the Origin of our Ideas of the Sublime and the Beautiful* appeared in 1757, and in 1759 he started the *Annual Register*, with Dodsley. Around this time he met Reynolds; their friendship lasted for thirty-four years until Reynolds's death, which left Burke heartbroken. His reputation as a conversationalist made him known to Garrick, another lifelong friend, who introduced him to Johnson on Christmas Day 1760. Johnson too thought his talk without equal, declaring that, 'If a man were to go by chance at the same time with Burke under a shed, to shun a shower, he would say "this is an extraordinary man"'. Burke was one of the original members of the Club, with his father-in-law Dr Nugent.

The Knight of the Woeful Countenance Going to Extirpate the National Assembly (EDMUND BURKE)
Attributed to Frederick George Byron, 1790

Burke was assistant to William Gerard Hamilton in Ireland from 1761 to 1764, and when the Whig Marquess of Rockingham became prime minister, he became his private secretary. In late 1765 he was elected to Parliament, making a powerful maiden speech. Johnson told Langton, 'Burke is a great man by Nature, and is expected soon to attain civil greatness', yet he never achieved high office since he supported the Opposition for most of the time, often in alliance with Charles James Fox.

Burke has been credited with moulding the Whigs into a proto-modern political party. His chief campaigns included the curtailment of royal influence over Parliament, his long attack on the conduct of the American war, and his championship of Free Trade with Ireland and Catholic emancipation, which lost him his Bristol seat in 1780. The following year he became MP for Malton in Yorkshire and in 1782 was made Paymaster of the Forces. (This year also, his son Richard (1758–94), known as 'the Whelp', was elected to the Club.) Soon Burke became involved in one of the greatest contemporary dramas, the impeachment of Warren Hastings for the East India Company's misdemeanours in India, acting as Hastings's prosecutor in the House of Lords for fourteen years. But Burke's most controversial period followed his *Reflections on the French Revolution* (1790), a passionate tirade against 'atheistical Jacobinism', which also defined a conservative 'organic' theory of British political philosophy and the constitution.

Burke's brilliance was undoubted, but his fanaticism made him enemies: in the Club, Burke was Johnson's one formidable rival in conversation. Despite his clever puns he was said to lack a sense of humour (he was very hurt when Boswell reported Johnson's remark, 'he is constantly attempting wit, but fails'). Fanny Burney was kinder – 'such spirit, such intelligence, so much energy when serious, so much pleasantry when sportive' – yet even she commented that in political discussions, 'his irritability is so terrible . . . that it gives immediately to his face the expression of a man who is going to defend himself from murderers'.

Burke's fiery obsessiveness was perhaps best caught by political caricaturists. The Byron cartoon shown here is one of many prompted by the *Reflections*, showing a Quixote-like Burke setting out from his publishers to tilt at the revolution with a spear made from his huge quill pen. Burke was a gift to satirists. About five foot ten and strikingly thin, he habitually wore a tight brown coat and a little bob-wig with curls and was immediately recognisable by his beaky nose and spectacles. He was short-sighted and often frowned and grimaced; he spoke harshly, with a heavy Irish accent, accompanied by violent gestures and fierce nodding of the head. Burke was noted for his extremes and superlatives and his sharp division of the world into friends and enemies; at times he seemed to see himself as the defender of Christian civilisation. He retired from Parliament after almost thirty years, in 1794.

OLIVER GOLDSMITH (?1730–1774)

Reynolds's sister Frances called his portrait of Goldsmith 'a very great likeness', but also 'the most flattered picture she ever knew her brother to have painted'. One of Frances's friends thought Goldsmith the ugliest man she knew, gawky, balding and chinless, a bit like a monkey, with his face pockmarked since childhood. He could be gauche, incoherent and tactless (the first time he dined at Streatham, he shocked Henry Thrale by asking how much he made a year), and his friends teased him mercilessly, as in Garrick's impromptu epitaph:

> *Here lies Nolly Goldsmith, for shortness call'd Noll,*
> *Who wrote like an Angel, but talked like poor Poll.*

One of five children of an Irish clergyman, Goldsmith studied at Trinity College, Dublin, and in Edinburgh, then drifted around Europe and tried doctoring and teaching before finally writing for booksellers. He was compulsively generous (often to people who did not need it). Thomas Percy found the thirty-year-old author of the fine-sounding *Enquiry into the Present State of Polite Learning* (1759) in a 'miserable dirty looking room', with a single chair, lending his meagre coal to a ragged neighbour. Through Percy, Goldsmith met Johnson, who was already impressed by his lively 'Chinese Letters', published as *Citizen of the World* in 1762. According to Boswell's famous story, Johnson once saved Goldsmith from the bailiffs by snatching up the manuscript of *The Vicar of Wakefield* (1766) and rushing it to the publisher. Reynolds was another stalwart friend. Convinced that Goldsmith was a 'man of genius', while admitting that 'others pronounced him an idiot inspired', he enjoyed his wayward humour and his passion for showy dress, and was deeply sympathetic to his vulnerability.

Goldsmith was a founder and key member of the Club. When the Royal Academy was founded in 1768 he was (half humorously) given the honorary post of Professor of Ancient History, and his unfulfilled proposal to edit a new dictionary of arts and sciences summed up the Club's shared, systematising aims – Reynolds would write on painting, Garrick on acting and so forth. Yet he remained poor and full of self-doubt, publishing a host of biographies and histories to pay his debts.

Reynolds catches Goldsmith's awkwardness, but he gives his friend dignity, with his fur-edged cloak. The coin-like profile follows a formal

OLIVER GOLDSMITH
Sir Joshua Reynolds, 1772

Renaissance convention, here signifying intellect, while the seventeenth-century style of his open collar and lace cuffs set him in a British intellectual tradition. The portrait was commissioned by the Duke of Dorset, with the companion portrait of *'Johnson arguing'*: the first version was exhibited at the Academy in 1770, and this copy was made for Streatham in 1772. The painting recognises Goldsmith's importance as a leading literary figure, who linked Augustan decorum to the new vogue for sensibility and humanity. Above all, it seemed, Goldsmith could find his own authentic voice in any genre: *The Traveller* (1764) was praised by Johnson as the finest poem since Alexander Pope; *The Vicar of Wakefield* rushed through three editions; the long, moving, yet generalised poem *The Deserted Village* (1770), dedicated to Reynolds, was followed by the rollicking comedy of *She Stoops to Conquer* (1773), which completely revitalised the old comedy of manners.

Goldsmith never married, although he was teased about his relationship with Mary Horneck, whom he accompanied to Paris with her mother and sister in 1770. He could be infuriating, but his oddity and warmth made him much loved. When he died, aged forty-four (still owing £2,000), his friends were distraught and his funeral was attended by sobbing crowds of the poor. Reynolds arranged for a monument in Westminster Abbey, paid for by the Club. It bore a medallion by Nollekens and a Latin inscription by Johnson.

JAMES BOSWELL (1740–95)

B oswell's fame rests on his *Life of Johnson*, but he was a dramatic, energetic, wildly contradictory character in his own right: his real subject
was himself – after a conversation with Johnson about Swift and Addison,
he adds happily 'We then talked of Me'.

JAMES BOSWELL, George Willison, 1765

Boswell came from an old Scottish family in Auchinleck, Ayrshire; his Presbyterian father became Lord of Court of Sessions in 1754. The eldest of three sons, he received a classical education in Edinburgh. Bashful, priggish and timid, he suffered a nervous collapse at seventeen, emerging a different person – vain, gregarious, theatre-loving and publishing verses in the *Scots Magazine*.

Despite being sent to study law in Glasgow, Boswell was determined to live in London, hoping a commission in the Foot Guards would lead to 'brilliant scenes of happiness'. Johnson had long been his hero, and although their first meeting in 1763 was daunting, Johnson soon fell for his flamboyance and flattery. Boswell immediately began to record his conversation, and while his friends tried to restrain him and his candour caused him considerable trouble, his sharp reporting and 'spontaneous' commentary made his writing vividly original. To Boswell, the Doctor, thirty-one years his senior, was not only a 'great man', but a father figure he could talk to about everything from religion to sex. Yet he rarely followed Johnson's advice about piety and the rational life, despite constant resolutions to stop 'rattling', to become 'solid'. In later life his drinking, gambling and insatiable sexual drive would lead to severe depressions and many disappointments.

In 1763 Boswell's father despatched him to Utrecht to study civil law. On his subsequent Continental tour he shamelessly bearded Rousseau and Voltaire and sailed to Corsica to meet the revolutionary General Paoli, another of his heroes. On his return he published his successful *Account of Corsica*, and appeared at Garrick's 1769 Stratford Jubilee clad as an armed Corsican chief. Boswell loved dressing up, and Willison's lush portrait shows him at his most dandified, aged twenty-five in Rome. Slightly plump, with dark hair, eyes and complexion, he wears a scarlet gold-embroidered waistcoat with fur-trimmed green cloak. Posed beneath a beady owl, he looks alert, his eyes nervous beneath their arched brows, and his face sensuous, with its inquisitive snub nose and full lips.

Boswell married his cousin Margaret Montgomerie in 1769, but although they had several children, he rarely stayed faithful to his wife, dividing his time between Edinburgh and London. Already friendly with Goldsmith and Reynolds, he was admitted to the Club in 1773. That year he persuaded Johnson to accompany him to the Hebrides, noting his own

JAMES BOSWELL
Sir Joshua Reynolds, 1785

glee: 'I compared myself to a dog who has got hold of a large piece of meat, and run away with it to a corner, where he may devour it in peace.'

When he inherited the family estates on his father's death in 1782, Boswell pushed desperately for political appointments. The failure of these hopes, and Johnson's death in 1784, left him in despair. In June 1785 he wrote to Reynolds, saying that he had so many debts he could not afford 'any expensive article of elegant luxury. But in the mean time, you may die, or I may die; and I should regret very much that there should not be at Auchinleck my portrait painted by sir Joshua Reynolds, with whom I have the felicity of living in social intimacy'. He proposed to pay for it over five years. Reynolds's portrait – a sharp contrast to the Willison – shows a middle-aged Boswell, who has given up the gay clothes of his youth for the respectable cloth coat and wig, its white powder visible on his shoulders.

To solve his debts and stay 'respectable' Boswell now published his *Tour to the Hebrides* (1791), an instant success. Next he set to work on the *Life*, dedicated to Reynolds and helped to the press by Edmund Malone's invaluable editorial advice. When finally published in 1791, it was an immediate, if controversial, triumph.

For the next few years Boswell drifted, until he was taken ill at a meeting of the Club in 1795 and died suddenly, a burnt out case at fifty-five. Maddening as he was, Boswell had real sincerity and an odd innocence. Malone wrote sadly, 'I shall miss him more and more every day . . . I used to grumble sometimes at his turbulence; but now miss and regret his noise and his hilarity and his perpetual good humour, which had no bounds.'

EDMUND MALONE (1741–1812)

The son of an Irish judge and MP, the quiet, scholarly Edmund Malone was the editor of Shakespeare, a pioneer historian of early English drama, and a biographer. He is interesting in the Club's formulation of a national cultural tradition because he believed so profoundly that archival research, biography and portraits (which he collected eagerly) were vital to scholarship.

Malone graduated in law from Trinity College in 1761, and two years later entered the Inner Temple, close to Johnson's lodgings. They met in 1764, when Malone was twenty-three and Johnson was finishing his edition of Shakespeare; when Malone published his own edition, he commented that Johnson's 'vigorous and comprehensive understanding threw more light on his authour than all his predecessors had done'. In

EDMUND MALONE, Sir Joshua Reynolds, 1778

1777 he edited Goldsmith's *Poems and Plays*, with a short memoir, and helped George Steevens with the third edition of Johnson's *Shakespeare* publishing his *Attempt to ascertain the Order . . .* of the plays in 1778 Reynolds painted his gentle, thoughtful portrait around this time, altering some details ten years later.

Malone joined the Club in 1782, taking the place left vacant as a mark of respect since Garrick's death in 1779. He was not a sparkling conversationalist but 'eminently clubbable' – a generous scholar from whom everyone asked help – and was the Club's treasurer until his death. Gentlemanly and mild, he could however be driven to fury by lax scholarship slights on Johnson, rows over Shakespearean editing and especially by forgery: he exposed Thomas Chatterton's 'Rowley' poems in 1782, and the Shakespeare forgeries of William Henry Ireland in 1795.

From the 1760s Malone almost hero-worshipped Johnson, calling him 'next to Shakespeare'; he collected Johnsoniana and wrote a detailed obituary in the *Gentleman's Magazine*. He read and revised Boswell's *Tour to the Hebrides* in 1785 and was a vital influence on Boswell's *Life*, helping him through his darkest moments, making him avoid women and wine and revising the final draft. As Boswell's literary executor, he edited the third to sixth editions between 1799 and 1811.

After seven years labour, Malone's ten-volume edition of Shakespeare plus biography, appeared in 1790. He now became a special friend of Reynolds, publishing his writings with a long account of his life in 1797 and after 1800 was particularly close to Charles Burney. Percy called him the 'great Corner Stone, or connecting cement' of the Club, carrying its traditions into a new century. When he died in 1812, Hester Thrale Piozzi wrote in her diary, 'Mr Malone dead in the Paper; poor Malone! last of the old set. Helas!'

HESTER LYNCH THRALE (1741–1821)

❦

Hester Thrale was one of Johnson's closest confidants; her *Anecdotes* and her journals, published as *Thraliana*, provide a vivid account of him and the group as a whole. Tiny, with pronounced features, a sharp nose and wide mouth, and large, muscular hands, she was not a beauty, but her wit, vivacity, learning and volatile emotions gave her an irresistible warmth. The daughter of a wealthy Welsh landowner, at twenty-one she reluctantly married Henry Thrale (?1729–81), a prosperous, ambitious brewer. Thrale had been to Oxford (where he met Arthur Murphy) and had lived a rakish life before inheriting the family brewery, with a town house in Southwark and a country home, Streatham Park.

For several years Hester was constantly pregnant and anxious about her children, but her literary interests were frustrated and she was delighted to meet Johnson in 1765. Johnson appreciated Hester's intelligence, teased her, argued with her, even translated Boethius with her; in turn, she flattered and amused him and nursed him devotedly after his near-breakdown in 1766. They both helped with Thrale's election campaigns – he was MP for Southwark from 1765–80 – and this revived Johnson's own political interest, expressed in four powerful pamphlets between 1770 and 1775.

With Johnson as a magnet, Hester became hostess to the Club. At Streatham Johnson rested, wrote, collected books for

HESTER LYNCH **Piozzi** (Mrs Thrale)
George Dance, 1793

55

the library, and built a brick furnace in the kitchen garden for scientific experiments until stopped by Thrale, alarmed at potential explosions. From 1774 he also travelled with the Thrales to Wales, France, Brighton and Bath. He became fond of the children, and over the years Hester put up with his domineering manner, constant tea-drinking and demands for her prayers by his sickbed, 'which required strength of body as well as of mind, so vehement were his manners, and his tones of voice so pathetic'. She also cared for him in the fantasies brought on by his sense of guilt and fear of madness.

In 1772, when Thrale faced bankruptcy after rash investments, Johnson helped Hester save the business. Ironically, the Thrales' social success was at its height: Reynolds was commissioned to paint thirteen pictures of their circle for the library. Hester's world widened: she was presented at Court, became friendly with Elizabeth Montagu and the Bluestockings, and with the young Fanny Burney.

Thrale, however, suffered two strokes, and lost his seat in Parliament; when he died of apoplexy in 1781, Johnson was one of his executors, helping to manage the brewery before its sale. Many hinted that Johnson and Hester would marry, but Johnson's last visits to Streatham were in autumn 1782. Meanwhile Hester became passionately attached to the Italian musician Gabriel Piozzi, whom she now employed as singing teacher. In 1782, when Hester told Johnson of her impending marriage, he replied ferociously that she was 'ignominiously married . . . God forgive your wickedness'. Hester replied with dignity, and Johnson, as so often, apologised profoundly, but spoke ferociously to Fanny Burney: 'I drive her quite from my mind. If I meet with one of her letters I burn it instantly . . . I never speak of her, and I desire never to hear of her more.' Although he later wrote to her pleadingly they never met again.

Encouraged by Johnson, Hester had recorded his behaviour and remarks, 'put down in a wild way just as I receiv'd or could catch'em'. In 1786 her *Anecdotes of the late Samuel Johnson LLD, During the Last Twenty Years of his Life* was published, the first edition selling out in a day. In 1788 came her *Letters*, unusual, thought Malone, in revealing a relaxed, informal Johnson in 'the undress of his mind'.

Hester's second marriage proved remarkably happy, and the calm pencil sketch by George Dance shows her during these years.

FANNY BURNEY (1752–1840)

🍎

Fanny Burney won fame as the author of *Evelina* (1778), a fast and funny account of an ingenue's trials in society, but she was also an incomparable diarist, rivalling Boswell in her records of conversation and sharp character sketches.

FRANCES D'ARBLAY (Fanny Burney), Edward Francis Burney, *c.*1784–5

The fourth child of Charles and Esther Burney, Fanny was a sensible, bookish child, who wrote from an early age. Shy, often embarrassed, she was five foot two, very short-sighted, with her father's pronounced nose, deep brow, expressive eyes and lips. In the portrait by her cousin Edward Francis Burney, her demure look is more than offset by the gleam in her eye – and the stupendous hat.

After *Evelina* was published Fanny was invited to Streatham Park, 'the most *Consequential* Day I have spent since my Birth', and her journals show Johnson – now sixty-eight, gouty, fat and often melancholy – in his most teasing and kindly aspect.

Fanny's second novel, *Cecilia*, appeared in 1782, but after Johnson died, and Mrs Thrale's re-marriage a different life began. From 1785 to 1791 she was Second Keeper of the Robes for Queen Charlotte, and in 1793 she startled her circle by marrying Alexandre D'Arblay, a French Catholic emigré. In financial difficulties, Fanny took up her pen again, with a tragedy, *Edwy and Edwiga* (1792) and a novel, *Camilla* (1796); her last novel, *The Wanderer*, appeared in 1814.

The D'Arblays were trapped in France by the war from 1802 to 1812, but eventually settled in Bath. After her husband died Fanny moved to London, and from 1832, when her entertaining *Memoirs* of her father were condemned as sentimental, she became a virtual recluse, a relic of a former age.

HANNAH MORE (1745–1833)

Hannah More was the daughter of a Bristol teacher, and taught herself at her older sisters' school, but after she received £200 compensation for a broken engagement she moved to London. Here she first became a successful tragic dramatist, with plays ranging from *A Search after Happiness* (1762) to *The Fatal Falsehood* (1779). When Garrick heard of her thrilled response to his acting, he invited her to meet him and soon decided they found in each other 'natural manners, original power, and wit, and in union with good nature'. Garrick showed her considerable help and kindness all his life.

The delightful silhouette combines a sense of feminine domesticity with More's role as a writer. She became a friend of Johnson, who always liked her, and of Elizabeth Montagu and the Bluestockings, but became drawn increasingly into the evangelical movement. Prompted by William Wilberforce, she and her sister opened a school in a mining area of Somerset, and turned from drama and poetry to essays, moral tracts and a strong didactic novel, *Coelebs in Search of a Wife* (1809).

At one point More made the 'milkmaid poet', Ann Yearsley, her protégée, insisting that this should not make Yearsley forget the duties of wife and mother. Despite her *Strictures on the Modern System of Female Education* (1799), her feminism was of a distinctly conservative kind.

HANNAH MORE, Augustin Edouart, 1827

EDWARD GIBBON (1737–94)

❧

The Decline and Fall of the Roman Empire, Edward Gibbon's masterpiece, offered both a model and a warning, a proud republic now a tumble of picturesque ruins. Thomas Carlyle saw it as a bridge 'swinging gorgeously across the gloomy and multitudinous chasm of those barbarous centuries'.

Gibbon visited Rome on his Grand Tour, when he was twenty-seven. The son of a wealthy MP, he was a sickly child – the only one of seven to survive. He found Oxford dull, ignorant, drunken and corrupt and in 1753, after becoming a (brief) romantic convert to Catholicism, he was packed off for five crucial years to Protestant Lausanne, where he studied philosophy and classical and European literature, and was briefly engaged to Suzanne Curchod, the future Madame Necker, mother of Madame de Staël.

Gibbon became MP for Liskeard in 1774. The first volume of *Decline and Fall* appeared in 1776, and six more slowly followed, decorated with his outspoken personal footnotes – a staggering narrative of twelve centuries of Roman history, vivid, scholarly, witty and imaginative.

He was elected to the Club in 1774, but got on better with Garrick and Reynolds than with Johnson, who found his urbanity irritating. Gibbon was a dandy, plump, short (under five foot tall) and always overdressed, with a languid manner, pouring forth elaborately composed speeches from a tiny round mouth. His vanity grew with his fame, but he was so kind and good natured that his friends forgave him – and this affectionate later sketch brings out all the humour of the man, and the period.

In 1783 he settled in Lausanne. There he finished his last volume in June 1787, feeling he had 'taken my everlasting leave of an old and agreeable companion'. He died on a visit to England in January 1794.

Ed. Gibbon the Historian in Militia Uniform, unknown artist, 1817–30

Ed Gibbon the Historian in Militia uniform

+ This is in my Walker Lady Holland hand writing Newspaper Cutting Sam Walker 1870 CF Hoga

SIR JOSEPH BANKS (1743–1820)

Reynolds's study of the eminent young botanist, painted in 1773, is one of his most vivid late portraits. Banks looks patrician, as he was, having inherited the family estates at Revesby, Lincolnshire, in 1761. Strong-willed and independent, at Eton Banks was thought idle until he decided to pursue botany instead of classics, learning from country-women who supplied herbs to local druggists. At Christ Church he brought in a teacher from Cambridge, the astronomer and botanist Israel Lyons: in 1766, aged twenty-three, he was elected a Fellow of the Royal Society. That year he sailed to Newfoundland to collect plants, and then accompanied James Cook on the *Endeavour*'s round-the-world voyage from 1768 to 1771. (Johnson was much taken by Banks's account of 'an extraordinary animal, the kangaroo', and in the Highlands in 1773, astonished his hosts by imitating it, bounding across the room holding out the tails of his huge brown coat.) Banks's last foray, in 1772, was to Iceland.

Banks joined the Club in 1778, when President of the Royal Society, a post he held until his death. Although he was scientific adviser to the king and directed the Kew plant-hunters, he constantly sent back to France valuable specimens from French expedition ships captured during the Napoleonic wars, declaring he 'would not steal a single botanic idea from those who had gone in peril of their lives to get them'. Autocratic despot at the Royal Society, his determination to give natural history equal status to mathematics caused a near mutiny in 1783–4, as 'treachery' to the sacred name of Newton. But although he wrote little himself, he was an inspiring patron of science, linking the systematising ideals of the Johnson circle to the research of the century to come.

SIR JOSEPH BANKS, Sir Joshua Reynolds, exhibited 1773

LIST OF ILLUSTRATIONS